★★★★★

MLB TEAMS

Los Angeles DODGERS

KENNY ABDO

abdobooks.com

Published by Abdo Zoom, a division of ABDO, P.O. Box 398166, Minneapolis, Minnesota 55439.

Printed in the United States of America, North Mankato, Minnesota.
102025
012026

Photo Credits: Alamy, AP Images, Getty Images, Shutterstock
Production Contributors: Kenny Abdo, Jennie Forsberg, Grace Hansen
Design Contributors: Candice Keimig, Neil Klinepier

Library of Congress Control Number: 2025936777

Publisher's Cataloging-in-Publication Data

Names: Abdo, Kenny, author.
Title: Los Angeles Dodgers / by Kenny Abdo
Description: Minneapolis, Minnesota : Abdo Zoom, 2026 | Series: MLB teams | Includes online resources and index.
Identifiers: ISBN 9798384940227 (lib. bdg.) | ISBN 9798384940982 (ebook) | ISBN 9798384941361 (read-to-me ebook)
Subjects: LCSH: Los Angeles Dodgers (Baseball team)--Juvenile literature. | Baseball teams--Juvenile literature. | Professional sports--Juvenile literature. | Sports franchises--Juvenile literature. | Major League Baseball (Organization)--Juvenile literature.
Classification: DDC 796.357--dc23

Table of CONTENTS

DODGERS

From their Brooklyn beginnings to the dazzling lights of Hollywood, the Los Angeles Dodgers never coast when it comes to the game of baseball.

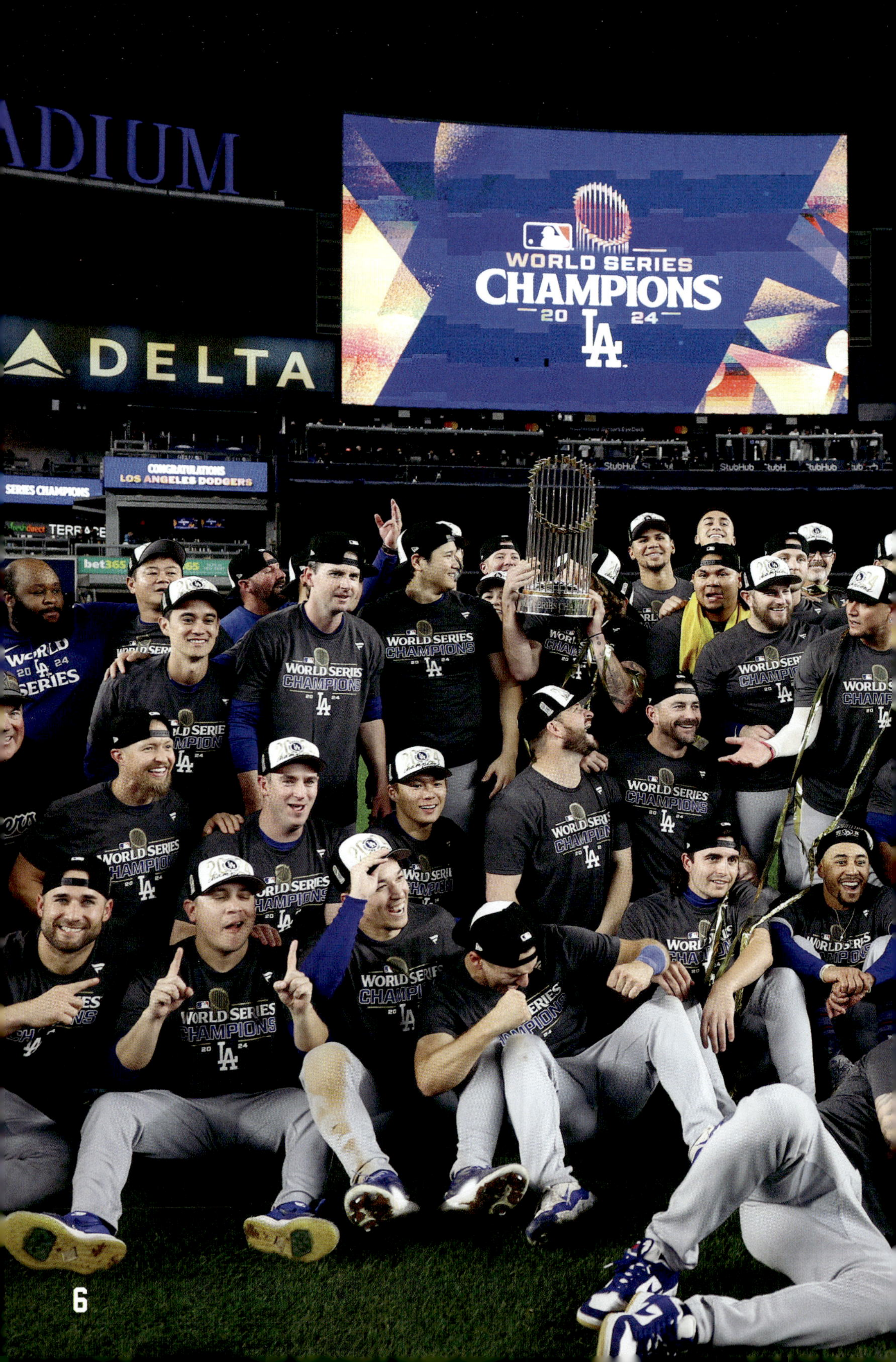
ADIUM
WORLD SERIES
CHAMPIONS
2024
LA
DELTA
CONGRATULATIONS
LOS ANGELES DODGERS
SERIES CHAMPIONS
TERRACE
bet365
StubHub
WORLD SERIES
CHAMPIONS
2024
LA

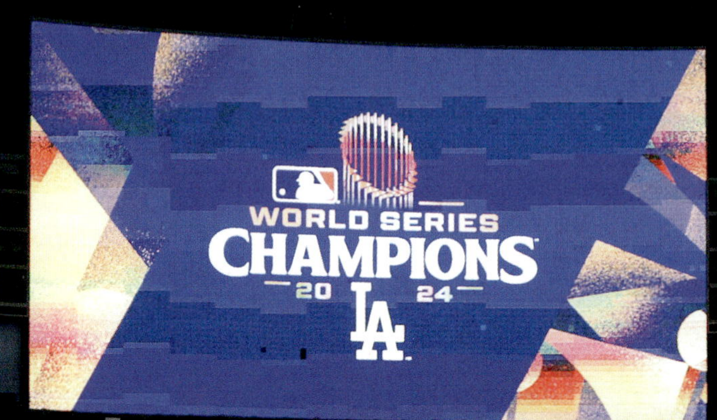

With legendary players, many World Series wins, and a history of big moments, this team always steals the show!

BATTER UP!

Baseball was very popular in New York City in the 1800s. Clubs popped up everywhere, including dozens in the borough of Brooklyn. One went on to be a professional team. Known by many names, the team started play in 1884 and joined the **National League** (**NL**) in 1890.

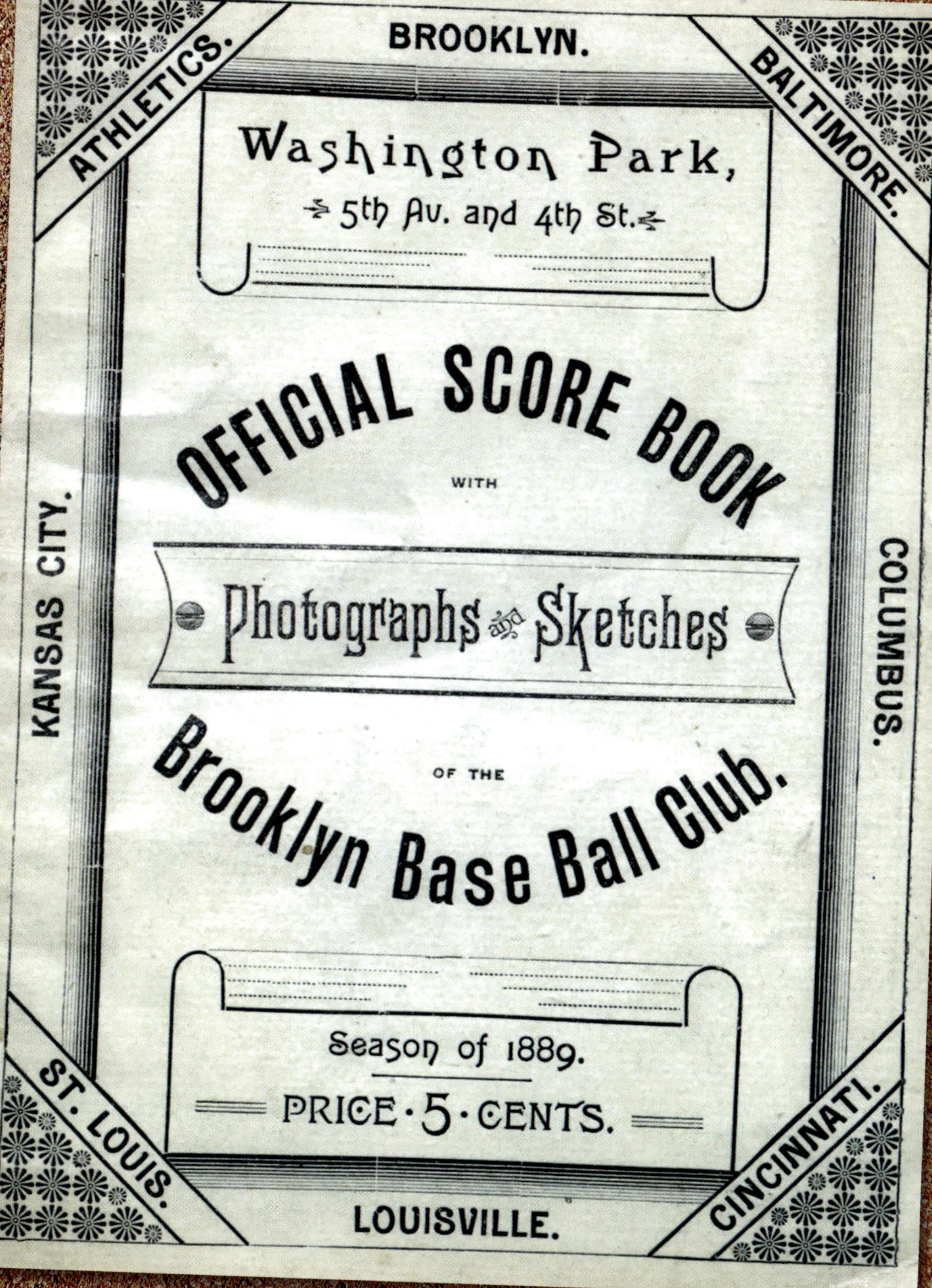
BROOKLYN.
ATHLETICS.
BALTIMORE.
Washington Park,
5th Av. and 4th St.
OFFICIAL SCORE BOOK
WITH
Photographs and Sketches
OF THE
Brooklyn Base Ball Club.
KANSAS CITY.
COLUMBUS.
Season of 1889.
PRICE · 5 · CENTS.
ST. LOUIS.
CINCINNATI.
LOUISVILLE.

Over time, the team picked up the nickname "Dodgers." The name came from fans dodging streetcars in Brooklyn. The team reached the World Series several times but kept losing to the Yankees.

In 1955, the Dodgers finally defeated the Yankees to win their first World Series!

The big win lit up Brooklyn and marked the start of a new chapter for the team.

GRAND SLAMS

In 1957, the Dodgers left New York and moved to California. The change did not slow the team down. In 1963, the Dodgers won another World Series by beating the Yankees again!

1965
Twins
Dodgers
OUT OF THIS WORLD SERIES
OFFICIAL SOUVENIR PROGRAM

In 1965, lefty pitcher Sandy Koufax helped lead the Dodgers to yet another World Series title. The team won the **NL pennant** in 1966, 1974, 1977, and 1978. Steve Garvey and Ron Cey were key power hitters in the late 1970s.

The Dodgers kept winning in the 1980s. In 1981, Cey helped defeat the Yankees in six games to win the World Series. In 1988, Kirk Gibson hit a **walk-off** home run in Game 1 of the World Series. The Dodgers moved on to defeat the Athletics in an **upset**!

LA
Dodgers

The Dodgers stayed in the spotlight through the 2000s. They won the **NL** West seven times in a row from 2013 to 2019. In 2017 and 2018, they reached the World Series but lost both times.

The Dodgers won the 2020 World Series, ending a title **drought** that began in 1988. In 2024, Mookie Betts and Freddie Freeman led the way. The Dodgers made it to the World Series against the Yankees and took the crown.

The Dodgers stayed strong in 2025. They finished the season 93–69 to move on to the **postseason**. Shohei Ohtani had a historic performance in Game 4 of the **NL** Championship Series when he hit three homers and recorded 10 strikeouts.

The Dodgers moved on to the World Series. The Blue Jays put up a fight with Los Angeles having to tie it up going into Game 7. Miguel Rojas hit a game-tying home run in the ninth. But the game winning home run came from Will Smith in the 11th. The Dodgers were champions once again.

HALL OF FAME

Jackie Robinson broke baseball's color barrier in 1947 while playing for the Dodgers. He changed the game and helped open the door for many others. Robinson won **Rookie** of the Year in 1947 and was named MVP in 1949.

Robinson was a six-time **All-Star**, top batter, and stolen-base master. He was named to the Baseball Hall of Fame in 1962.

Sandy Koufax was one of the greatest pitchers in baseball history. In the 1960s, he **upset** hitters with a blazing fastball and sharp curveball. He won three **Cy Young Awards** and threw four **no-hitters**, including a **perfect game**. Koufax helped the Dodgers win three World Series titles. He was named to the Hall of Fame in 1972.

LA
22
Wilson

Clayton Kershaw joined the Dodgers in 2008 and quickly became a star. He won three **Cy Young Awards** and the **NL** MVP in 2014. By 2017, he became the fastest pitcher to reach 2,000 strikeouts. Kershaw helped the Dodgers win the World Series in 2020. In 2025, he broke the team's strikeout **record** by reaching 3,000!

GLOSSARY

All-Star – an athlete named to the yearly baseball contest where top players from the American League (AL) and the NL compete against each other.

Cy Young Award – an award given to the best pitcher in the league that season.

drought – a long period when a team does not win a major title or playoff series.

National League (NL) – one of two 15-team leagues that make up MLB.

no-hitter – a game in which a pitcher doesn't allow any hits.

pennant – the title achieved by the team that wins its division or league championship.

perfect game – a complete game in which a team does not allow any batter to reach base.

postseason – the playoffs, including the wild-card round, divisional playoffs, league championship series, and World Series.

record – a top achievement by a player or team that no one has done before.

rookie – a professional athlete in his or her first season in a sport.

upset – an unexpected victory by a team.

walk-off – any victory in which the home team scores the winning run in the bottom of the final inning.

ONLINE RESOURCES

To learn more about the Los Angeles Dodgers, please visit **abdobooklinks.com** or scan this QR code. These links are routinely monitored and updated to provide the most current information available.

INDEX